Detailed Still

by Karen Neuberg

POETS WEAR PRADA • HOBOKEN, NJ

Detailed Still

First North American Publication 2009.

Copyright © 2009 Karen Neuberg

All rights reserved. Except for use in any review or for educational purposes, the reproduction or utilization of this work in whole or in part in any form by electronic, mechanical or other means, now known or hereafter invented, including xerography, photocopying and recording, or in any informational or retrieval system, is forbidden without the written permission of the publisher. Poets Wear Prada, 533 Bloomfield Street, Second Floor, Hoboken, New Jersey 07030.

http://pwpbooks.blogspot.com/

Grateful acknowledgement is made to the following publications where some of these poems have previously appeared:

Clockwise Cat, Diagram, Ditch, Elixir, Keyhole Magazine, Mannequin Envy and *Right Hand Pointing*.

ISBN 978-0-9817678-6-4

Printed in the U.S.A.

Front Cover Collage: Alan Neuberg
Author's Photo: Alan Neuberg

for Alan,
Liz & Jesse,
Gabe & Seth

Contents

Poem	*Page*
Science	**1**
Locomotion	**2**
Triptych with Corona	**3**
Tier	**6**
Detailed Still	**7**
Ants	**8**
The Bird	**9**
Orbits	**10**
What Returns Won't	**11**
Changing Coats	**12**
Good Times	**13**
Mouth	**14**
The Entire History of Your Fires	**15**
en route	**16**
Affixing	**18**

Acknowledgements

Science

Someone recalls an evening. The trajectory of memory rehydrates the event, pulling it out of an older faith, shaped like a set of urns aligned upon horizon's ledge. Someone might begin with imagination taking them to a chimerical establishment and credential events with precision. Stencil permutations to match light changing and capture nuance that was the moment that was. Unlike science which has met certain criteria and can be trusted to validate on its own terms, memory is shifty, wily, often unauthorized to present itself as anything more than an old coat that either still keeps you warm, or not.

Locomotion

Imagine if we could look at that first event on which all our future decisions about the way the world responds to us have been incrementally based. And imagine if this invisible chain between now and then could be captured with a time-exposure camera onto film small enough to view the entire progression

but also large enough to record it. If that were possible and we could clearly see the continuum of any one response, trace it backwards (this might require a crawling under, or regurgitating all the flowers we've ever smelled, or returning rooms to dark from switches pressed to bring light);

what we view might resemble Duchamp's *Nude Descending a Staircase*, or Muybridge's *Animal Locomotion*, or another variation, not yet done, not yet conceived, our very own; and we might get so caught up in the design we forget to return with full gaze upon our first face revealed from under what we have become.

Triptych with Corona

TRIPTYCH

(Center Panel) - **Fabric**

    muslin - or better - burlap
swatch, partly unwove, partly frayed-edge,
floating

… but not like an angel
(though in some lights, through some eyes…)

but more like something once attached,
detached

and about to un-dissolve.

It has been in the rain.
It has been before the fire.
It is the symbol on your breast.

(Left Wing) - **Fragment**

    solids - such as birch bark peeled and
curled, or veins like those on the back
of your grandmother's hands
    or less tangible - stairs leading up or
down, sun glinting off glass, toss
of a stranger's head

and suddenly:
love fills your eyes
love empties your eyes

(Right Wing) - **Flashback**

Would we do it again?
Again and again?

And what about the ones not kept?
Or the ones kept that don't rise

until unbidden, unrecalled, unexpected
hands outstretch, palms up and open,
offering
a time that is outside of time.

Can we have a taste?

Would we do it again?

Again and again?

How many times?

CORONA

Memory and Dream

One is a corruption.
On your screen parts slide
over each other exchanging acts.
Certainly lovers.

Tier

An erroneous flashback
builds the first step

of what becomes
the centerpiece of the entrance hall

in your house's home. Your base perception,
a holy ring inviolate.

Some days, you wake wondering
why you feel constricted,

but the busy takes the day
and soon you can't recall.

This, too, becomes a tier
under which you've buried something

you know,
but don't know what.

Detailed Still

A poem about my memory always begins as another day being extracted & displayed with fullest intention of ownership again reclaiming time now. My memory always tells me *go easy,* tells me *it was thus,* taking me in fully while I am not fooled and fall out. When I complain at such mistreatment, my memory steps back just far enough so it becomes a detailed still with inadequate distance and I cannot discern the precise manner of hands or exactly what anyone spoke. My memory will always end as it began, in a temporary shade about to be cast under light arriving from behind a cloud roving past sun.

Ants

Getting ready to stir up a memory can be like coming upon an inquisitive child holding a stick, studying an anthill. When the arm lifts, you intercede, admonishing with your tiny, Zen-bell voice. Fascinating as it might be, who wants such a scattering and its ensuing mayhem unsettling across the flowerbed, disoriented workers frantically trying to save the queen. She sits somewhere, deep, below, protecting the future, swollen with memory.

The Bird

This particular fragment – I'm ten –
seizes Spring outside my window – a yard of grass,
hedges, trees – three birch, a white oak,
and a black – captures
these as how it always was:
verdant and warm and full
of so much surprise.

This day, I saw a bird
fall from the white oak.
I rushed from my room, down
the flight of stairs, through dining
room and kitchen and out the back door.
Little bird lay still upon new grass.
I bent to touch, to feel for any sign
it lived, my hope to nurture back
to health in tissue-lined shoe box, to feed
it with a dropper, to one day have it fly

away. I touched blue-feathered back and wings
and turned it over. Out from within
what had been breast,
a mass of maggots crawled.
Backing away, I fled.
I did not bury it.

Burying was something I learned later.

Orbits

Memory can behave itself as though what it contains has the power to reproduce delicious pangs. As soon as you crave them, however, you find its body lacking and its mouth running off to someplace else. To assist, you suggest a trinity of excursions. At once, separate events lump into a globe surrounded by rotating rings, their orbits touching in a single spot, creating a road dense with briars. All that is visible are signs trembling with the reminder that memory is not the same as now.

What Returns Won't

What returns won't take you back
to anything - not the fields
you ran, not the sun,
not your father or mother
younger than you now
on the path ahead.

Their words won't reach
your ears - didn't then, won't now -
though then you knew for sure
their words encompassed
past and present and included
you and your brother
grinning and bickering behind.

And even if you should return
to that moment and begin
from there, you would
have no cognizance of the you
now; and you would rush again
ahead of it all, to be out of it all
before it was even done.

Changing Coats

Can you declare yourself another person and believe it for a visit's span? Combinations of several summers provide gist and drift. Discordant winters vie for credulity but keep changing coats, giving themselves away. You might begin with yourself wearing a red parka and playing in heaps of snow and immediately transfer into the school yard where you've undone your overcoat's top buttons despite the brisk wind. Here is where you don't know something about to happen never does, at least not in memory. But, how you had wished for it at the time, held your breath. Anticipation making you someone else while it lasted.

Good Times

The trouble, you tell me. But, I know
how this turns out; and so anything
I might conclude is looking backwards

into someone else. It could have taken
other routes – those of mountains, those
that veered onto dirt roads unmapped.

Did we play it safe only because
of fear? Our grandparents might be smiling
but they are still so lost in their own

confusion and fuss. Old people, having
arrived young from somewhere else they never
fully left. Dancing, like us, like we do

during these good times the disappointing disappears
and we manage to see what appears
to be a boat slowly sailing a summer lake

while the partygoers are all ours, all
intent on remembering this one way,
on forgetting it another.

Mouth

On this occasion, memory bathes itself on your inner mountain with a light older than day at sunrise. It promises a trigonometry of sensation, a performance of hands. Almost from nowhere, as though a magnifying glass was placed to enlarge detail, a cherished mouth appears, lingering over your surprised hunger. You find yourself looking into the oldest room in your life. And though you can place this in its exact spot, it disperses before delivering any content of desire.

The Entire History of Your Fires

The entire history of your fires
wedges between green logs
and ashes. Stale smoke ascending
into chaos scrapes
alongside you in sleep. You've seen
desire turn
into an old woman, seen it turn into
twenty songs depicting your entire story.
Dreams caught strolling up the sides
of memory, as if memory
was nothing more than just a chimney
emptying your past
into anonymity of sky.

en route

You're cruising the highway
that takes you from your house
to the beach,

and it's all sunny and expectant
within the car, whether you're with
your imperfect family

or a boy you wished had been
someone else instead. Or perhaps
you're pretending to be someone else,

someone who faced the ordinary
with spontaneity, who could feel
the music in front of strangers or sing

out from her throat so enchantingly
birds sat in her palms.
You were younger then

than you ever were again
except now, cruising
on the road, in the car, during

the ride into sleep. And some blessing
falls onto you. You become
all you have been and all

you haven't been,
each holding the other
lovingly in the car

of your body, of your heart, this person
you've been waiting for
who has been yours all along

going somewhere
you've never actually been
but yet somehow remember perfectly.

Affixing

Some days, you want to speak with a now dead one. You search doorways appearing like solid slices in a viscous panorama. As you pause to select *that one* *NO – that!* a different portal with different designs on you appears. Now you are rushing hither and fro within yourself trying to reclaim, trying to set landing somewhere past. Grandma attempts to assist you with steam from her chicken soup. Your mother sends the words from a poem she recited while sitting on the edge of your bed, tucking you in. Your father presents the stillness of the line between ocean and sky. You're left with no choice but to enter a memory in which everyone is present. Oh how they clap their hands at your arrival, surprise affixing their eyes on your unexpected face.

Acknowledgements

The author gratefully acknowledges the publications in which the following poems first appeared, sometimes in earlier versions and with different titles.

Clockwise Cat, "Science," "Detailed Still," "Changing Coats"
Diagram, "Triptych with Corona"
Ditch, "Orbits," "Mouth"
Elixir, "Locomotion"
Keyhole Magazine, "The Entire History of Your Fires," "What Returns Won't," "The Bird"
Mannequin Envy, "Good Times"
Right Hand Pointing, "Tier"

Special thanks to Molly Peacock, Dean Kostos, and Roxanne Hoffman.

www.ingramcontent.com/pod-product-compliance
Lightning Source LLC
Chambersburg PA
CBHW061519040426
42450CB00008B/1691